More Than A Bird

Liz Huntley

More Than A Bird

Salthouse Publishing

ISBN 978-0-692-49203-1

Scripture verses have been taken from the King James Version of the Holy Bible.

Photos in the text courtesy of the author, CCHS yearbook and Paul Braxton.

Back cover photo courtesy of Lightfoot, Franklin & White, LLC and Brandon Robbins.

Back cover passage written by Cole Peck.

Cover design by Marion Designs

Printed in the U.S.A.

To God be the Glory for all of the
special teachers,
both natural and spiritual,
that he placed in my life to direct my path.

Prologue

"Wow!" I thought to myself as I looked back. "How did I get here? God never ceases to amaze me!"

I had just spoken to a group of affluent women from across the state of Alabama who had joined the governor's wife at the governor's mansion for one of their annual devotional gatherings. I was asked to speak at the request of Alabama's First Lady Dianne Bentley after she heard my personal testimony to another audience while we were both advocating for high-quality, voluntary pre-kindergarten (pre-k) for Alabama's four year olds.

"I'm a long way from where I came from," I thought. More importantly, I had finally found an issue where my life could make a difference in the lives of impoverished/underprivileged children—children who share my past and with whom I could share my journey. I stood on the lawn as a 42-year-old woman, exceedingly blessed.

parents. As vocabulary is basic to academic success and IQ, many children are left behind long before walking into a public school.[3]

High-quality, voluntary pre-k is an effective early childhood education program that prepares children to succeed socially, emotionally, and academically in kindergarten and beyond. Graduates of a high-quality pre-k program are:

- More likely to graduate high school;
- More likely to attend college;
- More likely to succeed in the workforce;
- Less likely to commit a crime;
- And, less likely to rely on social welfare programs.[4]

This in turn leads to a more highly qualified, career-ready workforce equipped to take on the jobs of today and tomorrow. I am living proof of those results.

3 Hart, B. & Risley, T.R. (1995). Meaningful differences in everyday experiences of young American children. Baltimore, MD; Brookes.

4 Committee for Economic Development. (2006). "The Economic Promise of Investing in High-Quality Preschool." Washington, D. C.

Behold the fowls of the air, for they sow not, neither do they reap, nor gather into barns; yet your heavenly Father feedeth them. Are ye not much better than they?

Matthew 6:26 ***KJV***

"If God will take care of the fowls of the air, then He will certainly take care of His children because they are more than birds."

Pastor Elijah Good, author of
Moving from Insecurity to Confidence

Liz at age 5 before mother's death.

1

"Lawd have mercy," my paternal grandma shouted. "Oh my Lawd!"

I remember it like it was yesterday. I was visiting my grandma's house in the housing projects in rural Clanton, Alabama with my little sister, and we were playing in the back room. I heard the phone ring a few moments earlier, and the chaos that came after one phone call was scary. In an instant, with that one phone call, my life was changed forever. Although I did not know specifically what had happened, with the ruckus that was going on, I knew something horrible had happened. I dropped my toys and ran into the living room in the midst of the chaos.

All of the adults were crying, screaming and collapsing in great sorrow.

"Why would she do this?" someone yelled.

Even though I did not understand what was going on, the room was so small, and the grief was so contagious that I started to cry. My four-year-old little sister, Nichole, also started to cry.

Finally, my grandma broke the devastating news. She looked at me with great agony in her eyes and said, "Yo mama killed herself! She's gone baby, she's gone," she cried, hanging her head and moving it back and forth in disbelief. "She shot herself," she said as she continued to weep.

I stood there, five years old and frozen. Tears began to pour down my face like water from a faucet. I did not know what to think or how to feel. The adults were so wrapped up in the horror of the moment that no one seemed aware that a five-year-old little girl and her four siblings were now motherless. I just wanted to run to someone, to be held in someone's arms, but even in that small room, the adults seemed so far away. Standing there, I began to press the back of my body against the cold cinderblock wall and slowly slid down to the floor as if falling into a hole. I wrapped my arms around my legs and laid my head on my knees and sobbed.

***

When my mother committed suicide, I thought my wonderful world was being torn apart. I had a mother and a father who lived in the home with me.

I had four siblings, one brother and three sisters. Our home, to me, was nice and clean, and I had all the toys that I could want. However, because I was five, I did not understand that my life was only entering another chapter of chaos. The reality was that my siblings were the children of four different fathers. My mother and father were actually drug dealers, and that is why we had all of the toys and nice things. And my home was actually a housing project; one of the most violent in Huntsville, Alabama called Butler Terrace. Even worse, right before my mother's death, my father had been absent for a period of time. I do not remember what I was told about his absence, but he was actually serving time in jail for dealing drugs. He was released from jail within days before my mother's death, but he was not in a position to provide us a home.

I learned about my reality after my mother's death when the adults were sitting around talking about what to do with the five of us. No one sat down and explained anything to me. I had to put the facts together from listening to their conversations when they said things like, "She should have known that the drug dealing was going to catch up with them." Or, "She just couldn't handle it by herself when Willie (my father) went to jail." Some would say, "She did it to save her children because her lifestyle had gotten too dangerous for her." Some even still hold on to the theory that she was murdered.

A few weeks prior to committing suicide, my mother packed up the five of us and took us to visit family members for what we thought was a regular summer visit. My older brother Benny and oldest sister Debra were taken to my aunt BJ's house in Decatur, Alabama. My next oldest sister Pam was taken to my aunt Nannie Bell's house in Huntsville. And, my younger sister Nichole and I were taken to my paternal grandmother's house in Clanton, Alabama. Nichole and I had the same father. According to my aunt BJ, my mother explained in her suicide note that we were better off without her.

In order to cope with the reality that my mother had intentionally abandoned us with her suicide, I blamed my biological father. I decided in my mind that my mother was really a victim of my father who lured her into the drug-dealing lifestyle and that she could not handle the pressure of it all when he went to jail. I decided in my mind that he had gotten her addicted to heroin and that it was the drug that led her to suicide. However, as an adult, I learned that my mother had actually been the leader of their drug-dealing partnership and that she was smart, calculating and, if necessary, violent. She gave birth to my oldest sister when she was 15 years old and my youngest sister when she was 21. She was only 26 when she died. She had a reputation in the community that had earned her the title "Queen B" (her real name was Nannie Bee). It's not that my father was a victim. He was admittedly a willing participant. My mother was simply the brains behind the operation.

It is interesting to actually compare my personality traits to my mother's. She wanted the best for her children, she was smart and an influential person (albeit not in a positive way) in her community. Although I don't agree with it, she used her abilities to hustle for a living. I will never know if she thought it was the only option she had. However, I do know that she, like so many people in poverty, had the ability to do something positive with her life. Unfortunately, that was not the path she chose. I am just so thankful that, in spite of the painful experiences that got me here, God had another plan for my life.

– 2 –

Even though my mother's intentions for us were made known through her actions and the suicide note she left before her death, the placement of the five of us created a lot of chaos. I was so confused and not sure if I wanted to leave all that was familiar in Huntsville and live nearly three hours away from my siblings in Clanton with my grandma.

Our family members said that they would let us stay wherever we felt most comfortable. Because I struggled with my decision, I initially tried to live in Huntsville with my aunt BJ. However, the living situation was difficult because without the addition of my two older siblings and myself, Aunt BJ already had seven children of her own in a three-bedroom house.

After some time, I asked to go back to Clanton to live with my grandma. Although she had three of her own children at home, her house was not as crowded, and my little sister was there. So, at the ripe age of five, I headed to Clanton to my new home.

When I went to my grandma's house, I thought I was in a carefree and safe place. My grandma was demanding when it came to chores, but for the most part, it was a place where I could just be a kid—or so I thought. In those days, once the chores were done for the day, kids just roamed free in their communities and played with one another. Their play activities were not organized or even supervised. We would be several blocks away from home playing with friends for several hours each day. My grandmother just expected us home before sundown. In fact, if we were not home by sundown, she would stand at the corner of our street and begin yelling our names out loud. I remember being so embarrassed and running home behind trees and houses so that no one could see me and I could not see them laughing at me.

Unfortunately, with all of that freedom came the opportunity for predators to prey on innocent young children. In the first year of living with my grandmother, I recall several inappropriate encounters with older men throughout my neighborhood. Although I did not understand their advances at the time, they were strangers to me, and my grandma instructed me not to hang around men, and I managed to escape their advances by walking swiftly and telling them to leave me alone. I never got the impression that Grandma's instruction regarding men applied to the men in my home. My uncle John lived with us. For the most part he was quiet and paid very little attention to me and my little sister. But, because he was Grandma's son and lived with us, he seemed like a big brother to me. That was—until that dreaded day when my innocence was lost.

On one beautiful sunny day, I was out playing with friends and everyone wanted to get an "icee" or basically frozen Kool-Aid in a cup. There was a lady in our neighborhood who sold them from her refrigerator. We would just go to her back door and knock, give her a nickel, and tell her what flavor we wanted. It was so fun to go and get an icee after getting all hot and sweaty from playing several hours outdoors. I ran to my house one day to see if my grandma would give me a nickel for an icee. I went into the house and called her name, but she did not answer.

Uncle John emerged from his bedroom wearing nothing but shorts and said, "Mama's not here, gurl, stop that hollering!"

Upset that I was not going to get an icee, I hung my head and said, "I really wanted an icee."

Reaching into his pocket, Uncle John immediately said, "You want an icee?"

I perked up with excitement and said, "Yes, are you gonna give me the money?"

He motioned with his hand for me to go into his bedroom and said, "Come here then."

Although his demeanor seemed a little odd, I hesitantly followed him into his bedroom. When I walked in, he was sitting on his bed.

He said, "Shut the door."

As I shut the door, fear swelled up in my stomach, and I had a terrible feeling that something bad was about to happen. At that moment, Uncle John reminded me of those nasty men that had made inappropriate remarks to me in the neighborhood. The men that I had successfully avoided.

He then said, "If you do something for me, I will give you the money for an icee."

I wanted to run, I wanted to cry, I wanted to scream, but instead, I said, "What do you want me to do?"

He said, pointing down, "I want you to kiss me right here."

Tears began to roll down my face as I pressed my lips together, folded my arms over my chest, and began to shake my head back and forth to signify my terrified objection. I could not bring myself to speak.

He stood up and told me if I did not do as I was told he would kill me and my sister in our sleep. He said that if I told Grandma, she would not believe me and we would have to move out. With no other option in my five-year-old mind, I proceeded to do that which was disgusting while sobbing the entire time. When the revolting act was over, he reached out to give me the nickel and reminded me of his threats if I told anyone.

I threw the nickel onto the floor and ran out the house. I avoided my friends for the remainder of the day and hid out in the wooded area that surrounded our community park. I did not tell anyone. Life as a child was over. For the next five years, the encounters continued and the acts escalated to levels unimaginable.

– 3 –

Although we were poor, my grandma did the best she could with what she had to try to provide us a home. She had four basic things that she always preached to me and my sister. First, go to church. Second, obey your elders. Third, be a clean person. And fourth, get an education. So we attended church every Sunday, I was severely reprimanded at the slightest sign of disobedience, and our home in the projects was kept clean.

As for my education at the time, my grandma sent me to a neighborhood preschool held in the fellowship hall of Union Baptist Church. It was the mid-70s, and the county was experiencing the pains of the early years of racial integration in the schools. As a result, through a grant from the Community Action Program of Alabama, some leaders in our community decided to start a preschool program to make sure that the black children in our community were ready for school because they were afraid that the whites would make negative assumptions about the black children's ability to learn.

The preschool was several blocks away from our house, and my grandma sent me walking to school every day. She did not have to force me to go because I loved that place! Life at home was unpredictable and cruel, but at preschool, I got to be a kid and learn all kinds of things. The teachers taught us to read and write. Most importantly, they were so encouraging and gave us such praise when we made the slightest accomplishment.

I remember the first day of preschool like it was yesterday. When I walked into the room, I smiled because it was clean and full of bright colors. The chairs and tables were perfect for small people like me. Then, when the preschool teachers welcomed me with a warm hug and loving smile, I almost cried.

I teared up because, although I loved her dearly, my grandma was not a very affectionate person. I can't remember if my mother was affectionate, but I do remember that I longed for the warm and safe embrace of a maternal figure. The women at the preschool provided just that. I hungered for the positive attention so much that I excelled at everything that they put in front of me. It was such a wonderful escape from my daily nightmare. If preschool had not been a positive experience, my nightmare life would have extended beyond the walls of my home to another place where I had to "follow orders."

Sadly, the preschool program came to an end. I graduated at the top of my kindergarten class and was well-prepared for school. But I was headed into the unknown. Would the white people at the school across town be mean like I heard from eavesdropping on the conversations of the adults in my neighborhood? Was I as smart as the white children? After all, I had heard several black adults say that whites did not believe that blacks could be smart. They would say things like, "You know they don't want our children over there." Or, "Our poor children are going to be treated so badly over there." I was terrified because, at that point in my life, school was the only refuge God had provided me. Preschool was gone, and I had no idea what was going to happen when I headed across town to integrate into a new world.

Little did I know at the time that the teaching methods used by the church preschool gave me a foundation that made me more than ready for school. As an advocate for pre-k, I now know what high-quality pre-k looks like and my preschool had those characteristics. The learning standards were developmentally appropriate. The staff-to-child ratio of one teacher for every ten students created an environment where the teachers were able to give more personal time to each student. The creative learning stations recognized that children learned in different ways and challenged us with tasks that taught us to be creative. The structure and order of the classroom environment taught us how to behave and follow instructions. Most importantly, my preschool taught resilience.

The teachers instilled a "Don't give up!" philosophy in us by insisting that we figure out difficult tasks and not stop until they were completed. They simply refused to let us throw in the towel and give up on a challenge. These are all teaching practices that I observe now when I visit the high-quality pre-k classrooms in Alabama, and they remind me of how blessed I was to have been taught in a high-quality pre-k classroom before the term "high-quality pre-k" even existed.

– 4 –

I did not want to get out of my bed because the dreaded day finally arrived—the first day of first grade and public school. I woke up to the smell of my favorite breakfast: hot oatmeal with toast. It was my favorite because my grandma would let me add butter, sugar, and milk to my oatmeal, which made it taste like a sweet desert. After eating my breakfast, I got dressed in the new clothes that my grandma bought me for school. She got me several pairs of nice jeans and collared shirts. She had pressed and starched the clothes, and I felt good about my appearance when I looked in the mirror. My hair was in three very tight ponytails. Although I was a little nervous about my new adventure, I was having a good morning.

After eating breakfast and getting dressed, my grandma said to me, "Elizabeth, you get on that bus and go over to that school. You tell that teacher that she needs to put an X everywhere on the paperwork that I need to sign and send it home. I will sign it and send it back to school tomorrow."

Scared, I thought to myself, "She is about to send me to that school by myself!"

At the time, I had no idea what a big deal it was that my grandma had put me on a bus to go to a school across town in the midst of integration at just six years old. I just assumed it was the way it was supposed to be. I was terrified and really wanted someone to supervise me through this experience, but I did not dare question my grandma's instructions. I did as I was told and got on that bus.

The bus transported kids from grades 1-12. On that hot September morning, the bus was packed with kids and felt like a heat box. I got on the bus, took my seat, and did not say a word. Because there were older kids on my bus, I was terrified. They were rowdy and really picked on and bullied the younger kids. As I sat in my seat hot and scared, I was relieved when the bus was in motion and the soothing breeze of air entered the bus. But, as the bus crossed the railroad tracks that separated my neighborhood from the "other side of town," my heart began to race. As I sat and rehearsed what Grandma told me to tell the teacher silently to myself, someone hit me on the head and said out loud, "Gurl, yo fohead so big!" Several kids erupted in laughter. I just pressed myself down in my seat and did not say a word. I thought about it and realized that my forehead was bigger than normal.

Then, as a way to cope with the feeling of humiliation as the kids laughed and pointed, I said to myself, "The bigger the forehead, the bigger the brain." I learned from preschool that I was smart, and I was going to show them all.

After taking what seemed like the longest ride of my life, the bus finally made it to the elementary school. I followed the rest of the kids off the bus and walked into the door of the school. It was a beautiful school with bright colors and clean walls and floors. And, to me, it was huge!

I looked to the wall on my right and saw the words "First Grade." Because I learned to read at the preschool, I knew that it said first grade and that I was attending first grade.

Then, I noticed that there were several kids looking at the sheets on the first grade wall and would hear a parent say something like, "Look, sweetie, you are in Mrs. Jones's class." Then, they would head off into the first grade area for their classrooms.

So, I thought to myself, "I am going to the first grade, so my name should be on one of those lists."

Because of preschool, I knew how to read and write my name. So, I scrolled down several pages with my finger until I found my name. Once I saw it, I smiled but felt so anxious. "There is my name," I thought. "They know I am coming, and I am going to be in Mrs. Pam Jones's room," I whispered to myself with a secret smile as I headed to the room where I would begin my new adventure.

When I entered the room, I wasn't sure what to do. There were several parents in the room with the children exploring their new classroom. Some of the parents were reassuring the kids that appeared to be scared about attending school. The room was beautiful and decorated perfectly for six year olds. I stood in the doorway trying to decide what to do. Then I remembered the preschool teachers telling us, "You always sit in the front of the classroom, the kids that get in trouble sit in the back." So, I walked in and sat in the middle desk on the front row. As instructed in preschool, I made sure that I sat up straight in my desk. I sat there for several minutes.

Right as I was starting to feel uncomfortable, as if some of the people in the room were staring at me, a smiling woman walked up to my desk. She had brunette hair and, although her eyes were actually green, they looked blue to me. She was an attractive white woman, and I smiled as she approached because she reminded me of my favorite superhero, Wonder Woman, played by the beautiful brunette and blue-eyed actress, Lynda Carter. I actually thought in my little six-year-old mind, "Could this be? Is my teacher Wonder Woman?"

"Hello, young lady," she said in such a pleasant and calming voice. "What is your name?"

I panicked. The moment had finally come for me to meet my white teacher. I did not know a lot about white people and was confused about what to expect because of what people were saying in my neighborhood about the integration of the schools. So, without thinking before I spoke, I just blurted out the instructions from my grandma that I had rehearsed on the bus. "My name is Elizabeth Humphrey, and my grandma told me to tell you to put an X everywhere she needs to sign, and I will bring the paperwork back tomorrow," I said without taking a breath. I could almost hear my heart pounding in my chest.

She looked around and realized that I was alone and asked, "Well, Elizabeth Humphrey, how did you get in here?"

I explained how I found my name on the list and came inside her room. She stood there almost frozen with tears in her eyes. A lot could have happened at that moment. She could have called the Alabama Department of Human Resources and reported my grandma for sending me to school alone. She could have said something ugly about my grandma sending me to school by myself that would have gotten us off on the wrong foot. Instead, she leaned over, looked me in the face, placed her hand on top of mine and said, “Elizabeth Humphrey, you are going to be the brightest student I ever have!”

The racing of my heart turned from fear to excitement. This was going to be like preschool where I could thrive and maybe even get a hug or two. She gave me a tour of the room, showed me my “assigned” desk and made sure that I had all of the paperwork with an X marked next to the places where my grandmother needed to sign. Once again, God provided me a refuge.

5

Although school was a great refuge for nine months of the year, the summers were plagued by the full-time exposure to my reality. As a child in poverty, my summers were not enriched with camps, academic activities or vacations. Instead, we woke up every morning, did our chores, and were sent on our way to hang out with friends in the neighborhood. We would return home to eat lunch and were required to be back before sundown. Basically, we were unsupervised for nearly three months. I can recall being several miles away from home on many occasions without my grandmother having a clue. I also recall having to avoid the advances of male predators in our neighborhood. Because of the predators, I tried to stay with a group of peers throughout the day. I was afraid to be out in the streets alone. I remember longing for the structure of school and the stimulation of learning. I would get so bored during the summers, which would grow into depression. With that said, because I had never experienced a summer enriched by parent-planned activities, I really had no idea what I was missing. I just knew that there had to be something better.

In addition to hanging out with my neighborhood friends, there were some other bright spots to my summers. First, I got to visit my brother Benny and oldest sister Debra. My other older sister Pam lived with another aunt, and I did not get to see her very often. Because my grandmother could not drive and we had no transportation, summers were usually the only time that I got to see them. Benny and Debra lived over two hours away in Huntsville with my mother's sister Bettie Jean. My aunt Bettie Jean would drive to Clanton to pick up my sister and me so that we could visit for a few weeks. This was such a sacrifice for her because she struggled financially and was a single mother with eight children of her own at the time.

Basically, getting to visit Benny and Debra at my aunt Bettie Jean's three- bedroom house in which 11 people lived was our summer vacation. Ironically, due to what I was experiencing in my grandmother's home from Uncle John, I felt like I was in paradise at Aunt Bettie Jean's house. Aunt Bettie Jean gave us more normal childhood experiences like going to a movie or going to the mall. Those were things that I never got to do at my grandmother's house and were a big deal to someone in my situation. Most importantly, my aunt took an interest in my development by taking the time to provide me some positive life experiences. And, she was really the only family member from my mother's biological family with whom I had a relationship. I loved my aunt Bettie Jean dearly, and she remained an advocate for me and my siblings all of her life. She loved us as if we were her own children. Unfortunately, she died while I was writing this book. I miss her terribly.

In addition to getting to visit with my siblings, there were a few other bright spots during my early childhood summers. One of those bright spots was the neighborhood visit from the Book Mobile. In school, I learned to read on an advanced level such that the novels came to life and took me on a journey far away from my reality. During the summer, I tried to convince my grandmother to take me to the library to get books, but she refused. Because of her fear of white people, my grandmother did not venture over to the other side of the railroad tracks unless it was to pay bills or buy food and clothing. Fortunately, there was a truck that looked like an ice cream or food truck that would come to our neighborhood once a week during the summer and allow us to check out books. The books were donations, worn and torn by the affluent, but to me, the destitute, they were nothing short of treasures. I would run with joy after the Book Mobile when it would arrive on my street the same way that other children would run after the ice cream truck. But my truck offered something no frozen treat could. While other children pumped their bodies with sugar, I stimulated my mind, traveling to places no one around me could imagine going.

I recall a time when the Book Mobile really saved the day for me. I was really sad. I had just returned from visiting my siblings at Aunt Bettie Jean's house in Huntsville, and I was sitting on the front porch with nothing to occupy my time. I heard the Book Mobile coming down the street. I ran full-speed to get a book to take my mind off missing my siblings. I don't recall the man's name that operated the Book Mobile, but as I rushed up to the counter, he said to me with his usual friendly smile, "Well, Miss Elizabeth, what can I get for you today?"

I replied, "I need something that will take me on a long journey!"

"Well, let me see," he said putting his finger to his head, "I've got just the thing. You need to read a series."

Puzzled, I asked, "What's a series?"

He replied, "It is more than one book about the same characters and their many adventures."

I was so excited because it was just what I needed.

He went on, "And, I know just the series for you—*The Boxcar Children.*" Since we were limited to three books per checkout, he gave me the first three books of the series. *The Boxcar Children* was a series about the adventures of four orphaned siblings who lived with a grandparent. It was a perfect escape.

Although I do not recall its name, I was so thankful for the organization that provided the charitable service of the Book Mobile to my community and to all of those who donated their used books. This experience is why I am such a supporter of programs like the Alabama Literacy Council and other similar entities across the country. They recognize the value of reading for all individuals and its impact on their quality of life.

Another respite in my summers was a vacation bible school provided by a local church. The church congregation was predominately white, and would host a community-wide vacation bible school at the West End Park in our community. Despite integration of the schools, my town was very segregated. There was a city park where the white people would enjoy their activities, and the black people would have theirs at the West End Park. The blacks would only go over to the city park if they participated in any of the sporting events. With that said, it was very noticeable when the predominately white church would come into our community and set up vacation bible school at the West End Park. The church members would hang signs and hand out flyers to promote attendance to the vacation bible school. Although some black parents would not allow their children to go, I was on my own during the day and attended the program. It was held outside at the park during the cooler morning hours. The structure of the program reminded me of school, so naturally it drew me in. It also stimulated my interest in God. However, it only lasted a week. When it was over, the clouds of my life would return, this bright spot would vanish, and I would be sad once again.

A final bright spot in my summer was Mrs. Gussie Saxon's garage. Mrs. Saxon was a schoolteacher by profession and child advocate by heart. She lived in West End and started a summer school in her garage. Her informal program was open to any school-aged child in our community. It reminded me of a one-room schoolhouse. She borrowed desks and books from the local schools to set up her school house. We had to bring a notebook and pencils. She would review English and Math with each child based on their grade level. Although she was very rigid, she would always end our sessions with cookies and Kool-Aid. Some of the children would say that they only tolerated her program to get the treats at the end of class, but for me, the real treats were her lessons. We met a couple of days a week for a few weeks before school started. And, although she would hold the sessions in the morning hours, it would still get pretty hot during those summer months in that garage. The heat did not bother me at all. I relished the opportunity to learn and loved her for taking the time from her summer off and her own family to provide the program for us. She once told me that kids' brains go to sleep during the summer, and she started her program to wake up our brains before we started back to school. Although Mrs. Saxon has passed away, her legacy lives on through my life and the other lives that she touched during those summers.

We often hear the African proverb, "It takes a village to raise a child." I think that is especially true for children in poverty. The bright spots in my summers are true examples of that African proverb at work. When school is recessed for the summer for children in poverty, parents and guardians struggle with the need for extra food since they no longer have the meals provided by school and with the uncertainty of what to do with their children's time. Idle time during the summer for children in poverty can also lead to delinquency. I know this from my experience as a Guardian ad Litem for the juvenile court in my community for eight years. Our juvenile delinquency caseload consistently peaked during the summer months. Most of the time, the delinquent acts occurred when children were bored with nothing to do. I am not excusing their behavior, but I am using the information to show the value of summer programs like YMCA Day Camps, Boys' and Girls' Clubs, and other formal and informal community programs that fill that "idle" time for many children in poverty. My personal experience of having those much-needed positive "time-fillers" during the summer demonstrates how they make a difference.

– 6 –

The intervention of educational programs provided an important foundation and the tools needed for my long-term academic success. However, those programs could not cure my emotional struggles. The older I became, the more I understood the harshness of life. By age eight, I was severely depressed. I smiled and thrived during the day at school and returned home to darkness. I did not see the long-term value of education at that time. It was just an escape for me, and it was not enough to get rid of the demons in my head. All of that changed in third grade.

There was a new church in our neighborhood that everyone was buzzing about as being a different kind of church. My aunt Liz began to attend, and I noticed a difference in her. She seemed happier. She invited me to a service with her one Wednesday night. At that time, I attended church every Sunday with my grandmother, but never got much out of it. The preacher at my grandmother's church would stir up the congregation emotionally with his almost-musical performance. I could not understand most of what he was saying, nor could I hear it because of all of the emotional outbursts by the members of the congregation. With that said, I really did not want to go to church with Aunt Liz, but I welcomed any opportunity to get out of the house, especially at night.

Aunt Liz's church had converted a small neighborhood store into a church building. Red curtains hung in the windows, and you could not see inside. This made it mysterious to me. It was very different from the more-formal chapel-styled churches in our community. Instead of pews, the congregation sat in folding metal chairs.

When the service began, the minister, Pastor Elijah Good, asked the congregation to take out their Bibles. I had never attended a church where you were asked to follow along with the sermon by looking at your own Bible. I did not even own a Bible. The minister then asked for those who did not have a Bible to raise their hands so that one could be provided to them. He said that it was very important to him for us to see the Word of God for ourselves as he taught.

I eagerly raised my hand for a Bible. Reading the Bible and then comprehending what was being said reminded me of school and what I liked doing the most. I will never forget the sermon. It was about Joseph and how God used his life in spite of all of its tragic events. I sat and read along and thought, "If God can use Joseph's life for a good purpose even though all of those bad things happened to him, maybe He can use my life." What I thought were feelings of inspiration at the time were really feelings of conviction. When I walked into that church, I felt like a used rag doll. I was so depressed that I was on the verge of being suicidal. When I left that church, for the first time in my young life, I felt hope for my future. It was all that I could think about.

I could not wait to get back to the church the following Wednesday night to see what Pastor Good would teach. The sermon that night came from the scripture Matthew 6: 26 which reads:

> *Behold the fowls of the air, for they sow not, neither do they reap, nor gather into barns; yet your heavenly Father feedeth them. Are ye not much better than they?*

Pastor Good discussed how if God takes care of the birds and other things in nature, He will certainly take care of His children. He stressed that no matter what we are going through, we must be more than a bird and that God will see His children through any circumstance. As he kept saying, "You are more than a bird," my faith grew. At the end of service, I went up and professed my sins, and God saved my soul. I thank God for His mercy. When I left the church that night, I no longer felt like a used rag doll. I knew that no matter what happened, I was more than a bird and that God would take care of me.

From that night forward, I was at church every time I had the opportunity. For the first time in my life, someone taught me about life. Pastor Good and his wife were not just the leaders of our church, they became surrogate parents to me. They were examples of how to take care of a family and how to be contributing members of society.

Over time, my bond with Pastor Good and his wife grew stronger. Pastor Good constantly encouraged and challenged me by assigning me to speak before the church on various things from the Bible that we learned in Sunday school. He would spend time talking with me during our youth activities to learn about my thoughts and dreams for my future. He never thought any dream was too big. I recall telling him one time that I wanted to become the first black female president of the United States. The following Sunday, he preached a sermon about moving mountains. He asked me to stand up before the church and profess my goal of becoming the first black female president. He followed my public profession with a statement that I will never forget. He said, "And guess what, Elizabeth? I believe that you have the God-given talent and ability to be the first black female president of the United States because, with God, no mountain is too big to move and all things are possible." Although I no longer desire to become president, those words became a source of strength for me as I endeavored to achieve my goals.

Pastor Good and his wife regularly hosted activities for the youth in our church. For example, they would celebrate the academic accomplishments of the youth by taking those out to dinner who had made the academic honor roll at school. The dinner was at one of the nicer restaurants in town, and we had to dress well. For those of us who had the opportunity to attend the award dinners, it was such a treat. More importantly, it encouraged those who did not make the honor roll to strive toward that goal.

Pastor Good also knew that it was important for us to have organized recreational activities that took us outside our community. He would organize field trips to state nature parks, amusement parks, skating rinks and bowling alleys. For many of us, those field trips were the only time that we ventured outside of our town. Those field trips gave me a taste of enriching life experiences and created an appetite for a better quality of life.

Although becoming saved by God and being actively involved in the church did not immediately change my home circumstances, my faith gave me hope for a brighter future. I believed that God would work something good out of all that was bad in my life. That hope gave me the will to live.

– 7 –

When I started middle school, I began to more fully understand the severity of my home life and that getting an education was my key to escaping poverty. I was determined to make all A's on my report card. I was not sure how I was going to get to college, but I knew that having good grades was a start. I was pointed in this direction by my pastor and the teachers who constantly raved about how smart I was. Of course, no one knew of the harsh circumstances that were going on at home.

During this time, my tiny housing project home became increasingly strained. Uncle John continued to sexually abuse me, and I never knew when it was coming. Aunt Liz and her two young boys lived with us. And, my uncle Tim moved in with us.

Uncle Tim had spent time in the military and was discharged for medical reasons. When he returned home, he was diagnosed with paranoid schizophrenia. His behavior was scary to say the least. He would talk to himself and at times, claimed that spiders were in his head. Several of the kids in the neighborhood would make fun of him, and I was very embarrassed. Sometimes he would threaten violence, but Uncle John would get him under control. He could physically overpower Uncle Tim, and I believe Uncle Tim was afraid of Uncle John.

These were very confusing times. I was becoming a teenager and my body was going through a lot of changes. I started to like boys, but was not sure about how to handle those feelings in light of the abuse from Uncle John. My emotions were all over the place. I was on edge because I never knew what was going to happen at home each day.

In the midst of this chaos, church and school remained my escapes. When I was home, I buried myself in a book. I would even read during school between my classes or if I finished my homework during class. However, with no direction, I was not reading the type of books that I needed to read. I picked out books written by Stephen King because they were thrilling and I could become engulfed in them. When I was in the sixth grade, God used a teacher to point me toward the type of books that would teach me important lessons rather than simply serve as a distraction. Changing the type of books I read was a game-changer for me.

I will never forget the day that Mr. Art Smith changed my reading habits. Mr. Smith was my sixth grade history teacher. He was a very stern teacher, but I loved his class. He seemed to be particularly fond of me and often complimented me on my test performance and class participation. I always carried my library books with me and, apparently Mr. Smith took notice of the type of books I carried. As I was gathering my books and leaving class one day, Mr. Smith stopped me and asked, "Why do you read that crap all the time?"

I replied, "What do you mean, Mr. Smith?"

He said, "I just notice that you always have books with you that are about a bunch of scary crap. You need to stop reading that junk!" He went on to say, "Elizabeth, you are a bright kid with a lot of potential. You need to be reading biographies about people that did great things because I think you could do great things."

Those words of encouragement filled me with such joy. Although I had no idea what a biography was, I smiled at Mr. Smith for his confidence in me and said, "Thank you, Mr. Smith. I will get a biography to read."

As soon as I could get to the library, I asked our school librarian, Mrs. Alred, about biographies. She explained that they were books based on someone's real life story. I was intrigued. I had never thought about reading about the lives of others. It would be like reading about the characters in the Bible and being inspired by how they overcame life's obstacles. I read the back covers of several biographies and decided to start with Maya Angelou's autobiography, *I Know Why the Caged Bird Sings*. It was the perfect book at the perfect time for me. I related to Maya Angelou in so many ways, and it was such a motivation to read about the outcome of her life.

Although I continued to like Stephen King's books, I started to read biographies on a regular basis. Mr. Smith may not have realized it at the time, but his suggestion tuned me into the type of books that became a great source of inspiration and encouragement through some difficult times. For reasons unknown to me at the time, Mr. Smith was a true advocate for me.

I learned one day just how much he cared. When he would leave the room, he would put someone in charge to take names of those who talked. The punishment was two licks with his paddle. Usually, Mr. Smith would make me the name taker. However, on this day, he let another student take names. I talked when Mr. Smith left the room, and the student put my name on the list. When Mr. Smith returned, he went about his normal routine. He took the list and grabbed his paddle. He went to his door and called out the names of the students on the list. There were three names on the list that day. He called the first names out in his usual tone. He got to my name, raised his voice, and exclaimed, "Elizabeth Humphrey!"

I hung my head and said, "Yes, sir," as I made that dreaded walk to the door to accept my consequences.

He paddled the first two boys, and I jumped each time he gave them their licks. He sent the boys back into the classroom and there we stood in the hall together facing each other. Mr. Smith had a sad look on his face, and I thought he was about to cry. He looked me in the eyes and said, "You know that this is going to hurt me more than it is going to hurt you."

I was surprised by his reaction. When it dawned on me how much he cared, I was very sorry for disappointing him. It never happened again.

Another middle school teacher that God used as a game-changer for me was my seventh grade English teacher, Mrs. Myrtle Littleton. She was originally from England and spoke with a heavy accent. She really pushed me to develop my writing skills and often complimented me on my potential. I enjoyed her class until the day she became an enemy, at least I thought she was my enemy at that time in my life.

One day, I was unexpectedly called into the office for a conference and my grandmother was there. Even though I knew that I had done nothing wrong, my heart began to race with fear. If I had gotten into any trouble at school, I would suffer serious consequences with my grandmother at home.

It turned out that I was not in trouble at all. Instead, Mrs. Littleton called a conference with my grandmother to discuss my enrollment into speech therapy. Yes, she wanted me, one of the top students in the class, to attend speech therapy! I was appalled and confused. I blurted out, "How could you do this to me?" I began to imagine the embarrassment of the kids picking on me for going into a speech therapy class and got very angry. "You want me to talk white!" At that moment, my grandmother gave me a quick and stern look. I immediately retreated and went on to say in a softer tone, "Mrs. Littleton, I don't understand why you would put me in speech therapy. I am a smart student."

She replied, "You are a smart student, Elizabeth, and that is exactly why you need to be in speech therapy."

By way of background, I did speak using "Ebonics" or what is more commonly known as "ghetto" language. For example, instead of four, I said, "fo." Instead of "this and that," I said "dis and dat." However, in my mind at the time, I thought that I was just talking like what I thought was a normal black person. I was very proud of being black and was offended that Mrs. Littleton would want to change the way I spoke.

Mrs. Littleton went on to say to my grandmother, "Elizabeth has so much potential, and I am afraid that her full potential will be limited by her inability to verbally express herself. She speaks well with a good voice and presence, but she needs to pronounce her words properly. I am just trying to help her." So, contrary to my reservations, my grandmother consented to my enrollment in speech therapy.

Trapped in the speech therapy class for the remainder of the year, I had to find a way to make sure that my peers never found out. Fortunately, I had a good relationship with the school librarian, and she allowed me to enter my speech therapy sessions through the library so that no one would notice. If I had entered through the door from the hallway, I would have entered right in front of the main hangout area of the school. Thank goodness for Mrs. Alred!

Today, I can't thank Mrs. Littleton enough for what she did for me. My ability to speak well has been one of my greatest assets as an outspoken child advocate and zealous attorney. She was not trying to change who I was. I was wrong to believe that pronouncing words correctly was only done by white people.

Three years after completing speech therapy, I won a county-wide speech college scholarship contest sponsored by the Civitan Club and traveled to the state competition to represent my county. The Civitan Club board member that transported me to the state competition was a black female named Olivia Washington. Ironically, Mrs. Washington was one of the most proper-speaking women that I had ever met. She was also the head of the agency that funded the preschool that had such a huge impact on my life.

– 8 –

By the time I was thirteen, my faith had grown stronger. I knew in my heart that all things were possible with God. I wanted to exercise my faith by taking on a challenge and doing something uncharacteristic for a young teenager in my situation.

During middle school, I was introduced to extracurricular activities. The students that participated seemed to have a lot of fun. I wanted to participate, but I lacked the financial resources and transportation. I specifically wanted to be a cheerleader.

Most of the girls that made the school cheerleader squad got their training from the recreational cheer program at Clanton City Park. So, I decided to do recreational cheer first. I knew my grandmother would not be on board with my idea, so I had to find ways to eliminate the excuses that she would make about why I could not do it.

I talked to my friends to find out how to sign up for the program. I got the paperwork from the sponsor and asked about the cost. She told me that I could participate in their fundraisers to cover my costs. What she told me was music to my ears! Now, I just needed to find a ride.

I walked up the street to my cousin Emma's house. She was my grandmother's age. Cousin Emma had lived in big cities and knew how to get up and go places. She had her own car, and when we needed transportation, she would provide it. My grandmother could not drive. I explained my dilemma to Cousin Emma, and she agreed to drive me to the practices and the games. I was ready to make my pitch to my grandmother.

As expected, my grandmother resisted the idea. She said, "Now you know we can't afford something like that! And, how do you plan to get way across town to do it?"

I was ready and said, "Grandma, I talked to the cheer sponsor and she said that I could raise the money to cover the cost, and Cousin Emma said that she would take me—"

Before I could finish, she said, "I do not have the gas money to give Emma to take you back and forth across town to cheer! The answer is no!"

Dejected, I walked up to Cousin Emma's house and told her the sad news. She promised that she did not expect to receive any gas money to take me and that she would talk to my grandmother.

The next day, Cousin Emma convinced my grandmother to give me permission to participate in the program. As promised, I raised all of the costs so Grandmother did not have to pay for anything. In addition to participating in the fundraising projects offered by the cheer squad, I held a penny harvest. I collected bottles to sell for recycling and I helped a few elderly women clean their houses.

Cousin Emma got me where I needed to go. I enjoyed cheering so much, and it was fun to do something that just felt like being a regular teenage girl. It also got me out of the house during weekday evenings and on the weekend.

Later that year, it was time to try out for the school cheer squad. This is where I faced a harsh reality. To do things like try out for a cheer squad, I needed to be more prepared than I realized. I thought I could just go out there, learn the material and make the squad. However, as the tryout clinic progressed, I started to realize that several of the other girls jumped better than me and had mastered the material that I had not. I wondered, "What are they doing to get so good?" My confidence was shot, and it came as no surprise when I didn't make the cut.

Later I learned, that in addition to participating in recreational cheer, the girls that were really prepared received private lessons from older cheerleaders and attended clinics and cheer classes during tryouts to perfect their performance of the material. That level of preparation had a price tag, and there were no fundraisers for me to cover those costs. When I told my grandmother that I did not make the cheerleading squad, she was not surprised and told me that I should not have gotten my hopes up.

I did not want to give up on reaching my goal, so I decided to talk to an older cheerleader, Audrey Campbell. She was a great cheerleader, and she was black. I asked her to give me a list of things that I could do to improve my jumps and my cheer skills. Not only did she give me advice, she started to work with me on a regular basis to improve my skills. The following year, I made the squad.

When I made the squad, I could not wait to get home to tell my grandmother. I rushed in the door and yelled, "I made it! I made the school cheer squad!"

She looked stunned and said, "Well, you know we can't afford for you to cheer for the school."

I pleaded, "But Grandma, I can do fundraisers just like I did for the recreation league. Please don't make me quit! I promise it will not cost us anything."

She replied, "Okay, but if it starts to cost anything, we can't afford for you to do it."

With the mandate from my grandmother, the next day, I went to talk to my cheer sponsor Mrs. Judy Finlayson about my need to fundraise all of my costs. Mrs. Finlayson seemed concerned, but told me how much I would need to cover the costs. Not only did I raise enough money for my costs, I raised extra funds for the cheer squad account. When I brought in the money from the final fundraiser, Mrs. Finlayson beamed with pride. She told me, "I am so proud of you."

Mrs. Finlayson never made me feel like the cheerleader who could not afford to be on the squad. She treated us all the same. When she needed to explain something to me in a different way because I did not have a guardian who knew what to do, she always held those conversations privately. She never embarrassed me because of my home situation. There were even times when Cousin Emma was not able to pick me up, and Mrs. Finlayson would give me a ride home. She always said that she was happy to do it and that she wanted to help me because I wanted to help myself.

Once again, God had provided the resources needed for me to achieve a goal.

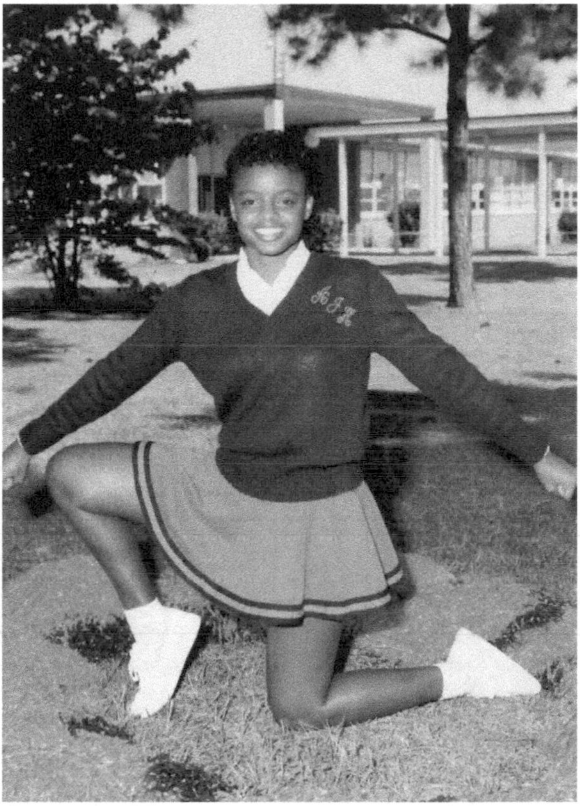

Liz's school cheerleader photo.

– 9 –

My eighth grade year brought about a lot of change in my life. The madness started right before school began. One hot summer night in August, I was up late watching TV in the living room. My grandmother, younger sister and Uncle Tim were asleep. We did not have an air conditioner, so I left the front door open to let in the cool air. We had a screen door to keep out the mosquitoes. I heard Uncle John approach the front porch. I no longer tensed up when he approached because he had not touched me since he discovered that I had started my menstrual period. I assumed it was over because he was scared that he might get me pregnant.

When he walked into the house that night, I immediately smelled alcohol. I took a quick glance at him, and he was smiling and humming a song. As I took the quick glance, we had a brief moment of eye contact. He had a strange look in his eyes, and suddenly I became very nervous. I felt the need to make a quick exit. I jumped up and said, "Do you want me to leave on the TV because I am going to bed."

He pushed me back down onto the sofa and said very firmly, "No, you are going to stay right here with me." He put on a very inappropriate movie, sat down very close to me and put his hand on my leg and laid his head on my shoulder. The alcohol on his breath almost made me vomit. I was in a total panic and did not know what to do.

Thankfully, my grandmother called from the back room and said, "Elizabeth, is that you still up? You know you should be in bed! Get in the bed right now!"

I had never been so happy to hear Grandma tell me to come to bed. "Yes, ma'am!" I yelled as I jumped up. As I rushed down the hall with my heart racing, I took a quick look back and saw Uncle John slumped over. He looked like he had passed out. Without even putting on my pajamas, I quickly got into my bed. I laid there crying. I thought it was over! "Here I go again," I said as I cried myself to sleep.

A few weeks later, school started back, and I had managed to avoid Uncle John. After school each day, I would keep myself busy and stay as close to my grandma as possible when I was in the house. I was determined that I would not be in a situation where I was alone with him again. I wanted it to end. In a manner least expected, the abuse officially came to an end.

I came home from school one day and my grandma was very upset. I asked, "What's wrong, Grandma?"

She replied with a shaking voice, "My baby was in a wreck, and they don't know if he is going to make it! It's bad!"

I was not sure who she was talking about, and I asked, "Who? Which baby?"

She said, "My baby boy, John."

I know this sounds horrible, but my entire body relaxed. I recalled taking a deep breath and letting out a big sigh of relief. First, I was relieved that she was not talking about one of my younger cousins or another relative that I loved. Second, I was relieved that, at least at that moment, I did not have to worry about Uncle John hurting me.

My grandma did not take my sigh as a sigh of relief, she thought I was grieving. She touched my hand and said, "It's gonna be okay. We are gonna go see him."

Inside, I yelled, "I don't want to see him!" But, I could not hurt my grandma any deeper than she was already hurting. She did not know that Uncle John had tortured me. I saw the fear in her eyes that she might lose her last born child and her baby boy. I replied, "Okay, Grandma, let's go."

When we arrived at the hospital, the doctors explained to my grandma that Uncle John was badly hurt. She rushed in immediately to see him in the intensive care unit. She was gone for a long time. We sat in the waiting room without saying a word. When my grandma returned, she collapsed saying, "He can't feel his legs! He can't feel his legs!"

The adults in the room began to discuss Uncle John's condition. The doctors were not sure if he was going to make it. If he did survive, they said he would be paralyzed from the waist down. He would never walk again. As much as my heart was hurting for my grandma, I leaped for joy inside because Uncle John was not going to be able to hurt me again.

This was such a confusing time for me. As a Christian, I did not want to wish anything bad on another human being. But when I thought of the years of torture that Uncle John had put me through, all I could feel was relief. I asked God to forgive me for how I felt. I recalled being taught at church that, if you want to be forgiven, you must first forgive. I knew what I had to do.

After several hours of waiting, the doctors allowed all of the family members to go back and see Uncle John. We were basically told to say our good-byes because they did not think he was going to make it. After the older adults had their visits, Grandma motioned for me to go back and have my turn to visit. As I headed back toward Uncle John's bed, we passed several very sick patients. Some of the patients were moaning, machines were beeping and making noises and people were crying. It was a terrible place to be.

I walked up to Uncle John's bed and Grandma stepped out and pulled the curtain. There I stood alone with the man who had hurt me so badly. He was lying there helpless and hurting. I said, "Uncle John?" He opened his eyes and they widened when he saw that it was me. Tears began to poor down his face. To my surprise, tears began to roll down my face too. I then did what I was taught by God's Word. I looked him in the eyes and said, "I forgive you." He lifted his hand as if he wanted me to grab it. I just could not bring myself to grab his hand. I just held my hand up as if to stop him and said, "Just know that I forgive you. We are both free." He put his hand down and tears continued to roll down his face.

I walked out and Grandma was waiting outside the curtain. She saw my tears, and I am sure that she thought I was just hurting for Uncle John. She put her hand on my shoulder and said, "It's gonna be okay, he's gonna be okay."

I looked at her and said, "Yes ma'am, it's gonna be okay." In time, I learned that it was not going to be okay.

— 10 —

With Uncle John out of the house, my mentally ill uncle Tim began to change. As stated earlier, I never realized it before, but Uncle John really controlled Uncle Tim when he would get in his violent rages. Uncle John could physically restrain Uncle Tim—my grandma, little sister and I could not.

Uncle Tim's mental condition was controlled with medication. After Uncle John was no longer present, it became harder and harder for Grandma to convince him to take his medication. When Uncle Tim did not take his medication, his behavior was out of control. He would throw things. He would kick us out of the house and lock the doors.

One day, he was in a great rage and went into the kitchen to grab a butcher's knife. He came into the living room where we were sitting and waved the knife at us. He told us that he was going to kill all of us that night. He pointed the knife at each of us individually and yelled, "I am going to kill you and you and you!" My grandma tried to remain calm and said, "Stop that, Tim, you ain't gonna kill nobody." When we went to bed that night, my sister and I were terrified. I did not sleep at all. Uncle Tim was pacing up and down the hallway talking to some imaginary person. He was cussing and fussing at his demons. It was a long night.

Although a part of me was scared to leave Grandma alone with Uncle Tim, I rushed out of the house to get to school the next morning. I was so tired and could barely keep my eyes open in class. One of my favorite teachers, Mrs. Jean Miller, asked, "Elizabeth, are you okay?"

I wanted to tell her, but I was afraid of what might happen if I did. I was afraid that the authorities would take me away from my grandma and my sister. I replied, "I'm fine, I just don't feel good today."

When I returned home from school, Uncle Tim was in an even greater rage. He was yelling loud enough for the neighbors to hear. He kicked us out of the house again and stood at the door threatening to kill us if we came back in. My grandma looked at us and said, "Come on, he will calm down."

We walked up the street to Cousin Emma's house. Cousin Emma advised my grandma to get Uncle Tim some help. My grandma assured her that he was okay and that he would be fine once he took his medicine.

We sat on the porch at Cousin Emma's house and saw Uncle Tim eventually leave. When he left, we went back home and Grandma locked Uncle Tim out. When he returned, he began screaming and cussing while he banged on the door. Someone must have called the police, because eventually several police cars pulled up with their lights and sirens on. We watched through the window as they tried to talk to Uncle Tim and calm him down, but he cursed at them and threatened to kill them. After some time, they physically restrained him and placed him in the police car.

Although I was relieved to have Uncle Tim brought under control, my heart ached for my grandma. As she hurt for her son, she yelled at the officers from the front door, "Please don't hurt him. He don't know no better!"

One of the officers responded, "Mrs. Braxton, he is just not safe right now. I promise you, we won't hurt him."

Although I hurt for my grandma and I dreaded how the kids might make fun of my situation the following day at school, that night, I slept like a baby. I had no Uncle John and no Uncle Tim to worry about. I thought to myself, "Tomorrow will bring what it brings, but tonight I will finally sleep in safety."

The next morning at the bus stop and on the bus, I could feel the kids staring at my sister and me. Some would even lean over and whisper to each other as we walked by. I sat next to my neighbor, Lanette. After several moments of silence, she asked, "Are y'all okay? I was scared for you last night."

I replied, "For now, we are okay."

We sat in silence for the remainder of the ride.

When we returned home from school, there was an unfamiliar car parked in our driveway. I felt my heart sink and could just sense that something was not right. I walked into the living room where my grandma and two white women were talking. The women had folders and paperwork in their laps. One of the women introduced herself and said that they were assigned as our social workers from the department of child services. They explained to us that, because of Uncle Tim, our home was unsafe and that we would need to leave our home for a while until they were sure that it was safe for us to return. My younger sister began to cry and scream that she did not want to leave. My grandma told us that we would have to go for now. So just like that, we went back to our rooms and packed up our clothes. We did not have luggage so we put our clothes in black garbage bags. My strong grandma looked so defeated and weak as she helped us pack in silence.

When we walked outside with our bags to leave with the social workers, people from the neighborhood were watching us from their front porches. My little sister was sobbing. My grandma stood in the doorway with tears rolling down her face. It was one of the worst moments of my life. We were headed to a foster home.

Fortunately, all foster homes are not bad places, and we were placed with a good foster parent named Ida Wilson. Even better, she lived in our neighborhood. We knew the other foster kids that had been with her for several years. When we arrived, they were clearly prepared to see us. They were extremely nice and took us to the bedroom that my sister and I would share. I was glad to see that there was only one bed so that I could sleep right next to my sister. That night we slept close together without saying a word. But before we went to sleep, knowing that I had to be strong for her, I looked at her and said, "It's gonna be alright."

Once again, the next day, we had to face the stares and whispers by our peers. Word of our situation spread like a wildfire. Although no one made fun of me directly, as I walked by my peers in the hallways of school, I felt like an animal in a cage at the zoo. I felt numb and for several days, just went through the motions.

Within a week, we came to Mrs. Wilson's house from school to find a pleasant surprise. We walked in the front door to find my aunt Bettie Jean. With her arms open, she said, "Hey, babies! Auntie is here." My sister and I leaped into her arms. She explained that she was there to take us to live with her while Grandma worked things out so that we could return home. Although we were treated like family at Mrs. Wilson's house and I was thankful for her, there was nothing like being with your real family. I wept with joy.

Aunt Bettie Jean took us by to visit Grandma before we headed to Huntsville. Grandma looked so sad. She told us that she was doing everything she could so the judge would let us come back home. Although she wasn't normally affectionate, she hugged us tightly for several minutes. She hugged Aunt Bettie Jean and thanked her for coming to get us. As we left, she said, "I promise I will get y'all back."

When we arrived at Aunt Bettie Jean's house, everyone was so happy to see us. It felt like one of our summer visits. After we were settled in for a few weeks, I realized that our presence was a hardship on Aunt Bettie Jean. She loved us like her own children and worked hard to provide for us. She lived in a decent neighborhood, and we were zoned for a decent school. However, as a single mom, she had to stretch every penny, and things were tight. During our summer visits, I was so busy enjoying our time together that I never noticed how stressed she was.

I had also hoped to get to spend time with my older brother and sister. Unfortunately, my older brother had become a drug dealer, and Aunt Bettie Jean did not allow him to come around. I rarely got to see my older sister because she had moved out and was a teenage mother of two boys.

I missed my church and my school. I wanted to go home. After a few months, the court found that Uncle Tim was stable, and we were able to return home. However, from that time forward, my teenage life was a rollercoaster ride of unpredictable turns. Uncle Tim's violent episodes continued, and we would have to leave again until he was brought under control.

I could not have survived that time without the Word of God and encouragement from my pastor. I learned how to endure the bad times because I had hope for a better future in my adult life.

11

The summer after my eighth grade year, I began my first job. The city of Clanton had a summer job program for low-income youth where they paid their salary to work at an organization that needed extra staff. I was placed at the summer YMCA day camp as a camp counselor-in-training. If I did a good job, I would be able to come back and work there each summer through the program. The counselor positions were highly regarded by the community, and several teenagers interviewed for the limited number of counselor spots available. Without the city's summer job program, I am not sure I would have been hired. Also, I am sure that my pastor being on the founding board of the YMCA helped too. Once again, God used the tools of a program set up to give good opportunities to those less fortunate to help me.

Working at the YMCA helped me in so many ways. I finally had something to do with my time during the summer. It did not bother me that the day camp was located nearly four miles across the other side of town from my home. Although we did not have a car, I was determined to get there. So, I walked every day to and from work regardless of the weather.

I will never forget getting my first paycheck. For a kid who was as poor as I was, I felt like I had won the lottery. There were so many things that I wanted like clothes, a watch and a stereo. But I knew that it would not be smart to just spend it without a plan. So, I remembered what I had been taught in church—tithe, don't owe anybody, save and then get a little something for yourself. So, I took out my tithes to give at church and saved some of the money in a sock that I had hidden in my bedroom. With the rest of the money, I wanted to get something that I really needed. I bought a used bike to get me to and from work each day. I was so proud of that bike because it was my first purchase with my own money. It was my first experience of the ability to improve my quality of life. It was very tiring to end my work day with a long walk home, and I had to get up extra early to make the walk to work. With the bicycle, I was able to get there in a few minutes and was not tired at all.

The bike was not a top-of-the-line bike. In fact, the kids in the neighborhood made fun of it. I did not care, because it provided me something that I needed. I even had a name for it—Blue Bell. It was an old blue bike with big wheels. It had a metal basket in front and a bell on the handle bars. I recall announcing my arrival to camp every morning by ringing my bell when I rode up to the building.

Although it certainly did not make me rich, the money I earned while working gave me the opportunity to get some things that I would not have been able to get otherwise. Earning money also made me excited about my future. I began to regard my education as even more important. If I had a good education, I could get a good job and earn more money.

And, although I was spiritually aware that money alone could not make you happy, it certainly could improve the quality of my natural life here on earth. Even more importantly, I realized that earning money could someday put me in a position to help somebody the way people had helped me.

Not only did working at the YMCA help me earn money, it helped me develop as a person. We went to camp for training to become good counselors. I learned so much from those experiences. It also gave me the opportunity for travel. I had never experienced a real vacation. Going to the training camps and our end-of-summer camp counselor beach trips were huge treats for me. It was the first time that I had ever been to a beach. Those types of experiences were life-changing because, like getting the taste of earning an income, exposure to places like the beach and camps in the mountains will make you want to have more of those experiences. I never knew how much fun life could be.

I loved the job at the YMCA and really worked hard to make a good impression because I wanted to be hired back each summer. My hard work paid off, and I not only worked at the day camp through the summer job program, I was eventually hired directly by the YMCA to work at their afterschool program.

The most important treasures I gained from my work experience at the YMCA were the lifelong friendships that I now have with some of the other camp counselors. Adults are not the only people that can impact a child's life. Sometimes, the greatest influence on a child is another child.

The YMCA hired counselors that had good character. My best friend Monica was one of those hired. Monica was beautiful and popular. But more importantly, she was and is beautiful on the inside. She knew about all of the things that I was going through at home. I was ashamed of my home life and did not want anyone to know. It was so good that I was able to talk to someone who would not tell others and who would encourage me. I will always cherish her friendship. She and I became close with some of the other counselors, and that group of positive teenagers established a solid peer group for me in high school. Having those relationships was like having an extended family.

One friend in particular was Barry Franks. We called him "Bear." He was a quiet guy, but smart and kind. We would pick on Bear sometimes because his personality really did not fit that of a traditional camp counselor. We were trained to sing, lead devotions and play with the kids. Bear was not very outgoing, but he was the guy that worked hard and would help get things done.

I often led the morning devotion for camp. One day, Bear asked me about my spiritual life. He was somewhat aware of my home life, and he said that he was impressed with my positive outlook on life. He wanted to know more about God. So, I witnessed to him and invited him to church. He eventually professed to Christ. Bear was and is now like a brother to me. We have been there for each other through some difficult times. He certainly came to my rescue several times when I did not have an adult that I could call on. God always put the right people in my path.

– 12 –

Starting high school was like starting a new chapter in life. My grandma had relaxed a little and gave me more freedom to hang out with friends. As for boys, she held firm to her position that I could not date until I was sixteen. Although I wanted a boyfriend like other girls my age, I struggled with the desire to feel pretty and liked by boys, on one hand, and the fear of what a relationship with a boy could do to my future, on the other. Also, my history with Uncle John left me completely confused about relationships between boys and girls. My grandma did not talk to me about relationships with boys. Everything I knew about relationships with boys came from my peers and church. Most of the girls my age encouraged an intimate relationship with boys, while my pastor and grandma insisted that boys my age were only interested in one thing.

I was so afraid of ending up pregnant like many of my family members. My aunt Liz was a teenage mother. My older sister was a teenage mother. I witnessed my grandma and my aunt Bettie Jean struggle as single moms. I knew that if I got pregnant, I might ruin my chance of getting out of poverty and doing something with my life.

Right after I turned 16 years old and was finally able to date boys, something happened that really put me on my toes. My younger sister had a child. She was just a child herself at the young age of 14 when she became pregnant. She delivered the baby when she was 15 years old. The pregnancy and especially the delivery of the baby really took a toll on her physically and emotionally. The father was only 15 years old, and for several years, he denied that the child was his. To make matters worse, our fixed income required my grandma to come up with several hundred dollars to pay for my sister and the baby's medical care. To help out, I gave her the money that I had been saving toward a car.

My sister delivered a baby girl that she named Meghann. I will never forget seeing the baby for the first time at the hospital. She was so beautiful and perfect. I loved her instantly. I also hurt for her because my sister was so young and certainly not prepared to raise a child. And I hurt for my grandma, who now had to provide for another person in our home.

My sister was so physically sick after Meghann was born that my grandma and I had to help with the around-the-clock care that has to be given to an infant. I remember falling asleep at school and work because of being up at night for Meghann's late night and early morning feedings. It was a lot for me to handle as a young aunt who knew nothing about childrearing. I cannot imagine how much it affected my sister.

With our new family addition, I received firsthand experience of the huge amount of responsibility it takes to take care of a child. And, as tired as I was, I loved that little girl with all of my heart. Her big, bright eyes beamed with curiosity. Her smile was like therapy. I made a pledge to her that I would always be there for her if she needed me.

I would look at her and dream of the day when I could have a child like her to love and share with my husband. I must admit that the prospect of a normal life with a husband was just a dream for me at the time. Because of my experience with Uncle John, I wasn't certain if I would ever have a healthy relationship with a man. And, because of what happened with my mother, I wasn't sure if I would even know how to be a good mother. I just trusted God that he would work it out for me.

– 13 –

During high school, my time was mostly spent at school, church or work. In addition to working at the YMCA, I took on another job at Wal-Mart. I needed the extra cash because I was involved in extracurricular activities at school that required money. I also took my pastor's advice to keep myself busy. In my small town, there wasn't much to do.

I started to date boys, but I did not want to wrap all of my time up with them. Not to mention, I had friends that spent time with me like Monica, Bear and my pastor's daughter Mildred. They were always encouraging me to stay focused on my goals. I know that God put them in my life to help me get through several times where I needed a little help to keep moving forward.

It always seemed like bad news would blindside me and knock me down. I recall coming home from school one day to learn that my only brother, Bennie, was dead. He drowned at the age of 19. As usual in my home, no one knew how to deal with the grief. Everyone was talking about Bennie's lifestyle with drugs. I was so angry. I went to work and my friend Bear gave me a ride home. He sensed that I was upset and asked me what was wrong. I told him what happened. His first response was, "Wow!" From the way he said it, I knew that he wasn't acknowledging his death with the same indifference, that it was not just some simple incident, but that it was a big deal that my brother had died. He knew that such news, regardless of my brother's lifestyle, hurt me deeply. He then asked, "I'll bet he was a cool guy. What was he like?"

I looked at him and said, "Bear, I know he did drugs, but he was not a bad guy. He was just a hurt guy!" I sat there in Bear's car for several minutes talking about Bennie's fun-loving personality, his affection for small kids and the way he loved to play jokes on people. I talked about how Bennie was really a bright guy who could have used his intelligence to do something positive instead of living the life he lived. I was able to sit with Bear and remember Bennie as my brother and not a thug. Bear gave me a hug and I cried. Unlike when I learned of my mother's death, Bear's kindness had given me a moment to lean on someone while I experienced personal grief.

I was also blindsided by social services whenever someone in my neighborhood would report that Uncle Tim was out of control. I recall being called to the office one day during school. My social workers were waiting for me in the counselor's office. One of the worker's said, "Elizabeth, we know that Tim is at it again, and we can't let y'all go back home until things settle down."

I remember getting so angry and blurting out, "Why do y'all have to be so cruel! I am at school! I am trying so hard to do the right thing, and you just came here and got me out of class to tell me this! I know my home is screwed up, but it's all I have." I shook my head, resigned and said, "I can call somebody to get us until Uncle Tim gets out."

I called my pastor's daughter, Mildred. She had become like a big sister to me. She called Aunt Liz who came and got us. Aunt Liz and her future husband, Jerome, took us to a hotel for a couple of days until Uncle Tim was sent away for treatment.

During that same time, I had won a local pageant which required me to represent my county at the state level. I told Mildred that there was no way I could participate at the state level and that I would have to tell the organizers that they needed to send the first runner-up in my place. Mildred insisted that I go. So, she went to my grandma and offered to take me. She took time off her job and away from her husband to attend the two-day state pageant with me. Although I didn't win at the state level, Mildred reminded me that God would always provide a way using those compassionate people close to me.

– 14 –

Even though I had accepted my life and environment for what it was, I still had a fantasy of my biological father getting his life together and coming home to be a part of our life. Instead, he continued to live a life that repeatedly landed him in jail. While he was in jail, he would write and call us. He would promise that things were going to be better when he got out. Sadly, each time that he was released from prison, he would come and stay with us for a few days and then leave for the lifestyle that put him in jail. As I grew older, I told myself that I would no longer fall for his promises.

Even with my guard up, my desire to have him as an active father almost got me in serious trouble. Once, he was released from jail and actually moved in with us. He worked odd jobs. He helped around the house. He had been with us for several weeks and I began to let my guard down and enjoy my father being a part of my life.

I was working at Wal-Mart as a people greeter. One of my responsibilities as a greeter was to watch out for thieves. In my small community, I could usually identify the people that regularly attempted to steal. I would give the appropriate Wal-Mart security person the code to put the employees on alert that a potential shoplifter had entered the store. Several times, surveillance would catch the shoplifters.

My biological father regularly stopped by to visit with me while I was working at Wal-Mart. He seemed so interested in what was going on in my life. The conversations with him made me happy. It felt good to know that he took the time to stop by and check on me. Or at least I thought that was what he was doing.

One day, I saw him talking to one of the regular Wal-Mart shoplifters in the neighborhood. I witnessed the shoplifter hand him a full black garbage bag. My heart sank because I knew he was slipping back into his life of crime. My heart was crushed when I realized that he was using me to do it.

I planned to talk to him about it the next time that he came by to visit me at work. When he came by, he began to ask me about school and other things. As he was talking, I noticed something that I hadn't before. One of the regular shoplifters slipped past us as I was talking to him. I thought, "That is what he is doing. He is distracting me so that I don't notice the shoplifters and will talk with me until they get in and out of the store with the stolen merchandise." I was furious!

I made a decision at that moment that I was not going to let him continue to use me that way. So, I went along with his conversation while watching for the shoplifter's attempt to exit. When the shoplifter started to exit, I looked my biological father in the face as I called for security. Our eyes said it all. He knew that I had uncovered his scheme of using me to further his shoplifting.

While the shoplifter was being apprehended by security, my biological father abruptly left the store. Although embarrassed, I told my store manager what had happened because I did not want him to think that I was a part of the scheme.

When I got home from work that night, he was waiting for me in the living room. I yelled at him, "How could you do that to me?"

He responded in a way that I did not expect. He was not remorseful, he was angry. He looked back at me and said angrily, "How could I do that to you! You almost got me busted today! Are you trying to send me back to jail?"

I could not believe what I was hearing. My grandma asked, "What in the world is going on?"

I immediately responded saying, "Grandma, that man almost made me lose my job! He was distracting me so that his crew could steal from Wal-Mart!"

He immediately leaped for me and said, "It's time for me to put you in your place!"

Before he could get to me, my grandma intervened and told him, "Willie, you ain't gonna put a hand on her!" My grandma rushed into the kitchen and grabbed a cast iron skillet. She yelled at him and said, "Now you get your stuff and get out of here!" He tried to say something, and she interrupted, "Get out!"

He grabbed his stuff and left without saying another word. I will never forget how afraid I was when he leapt toward me. I thought he was going to kill me. I cried myself to sleep that night thinking, "How could a father do that to his own daughter?" Because of the shoplifting incident, I no longer saw him as a father. From that point forward, I referred to him as my "biological" father. The next time I spoke to him, he was in jail again.

Thank goodness the store manager did not hold the shoplifting incident against me. I won the $5000 employee cash scholarship my senior year.

– 15 –

After the terrible experience with my biological father, I became more determined than ever to go to college and escape my painful environment. I still did not know how I was going to get to college or whether I would even be able to handle it.

One day, a teacher told me about the Upward Bound program. She explained that it was a college preparatory program for low-income and potential first- generation college students. The goal was to introduce us to a college environment. Once again, God used people to provide a resource to help me advance toward my goal.

The program was held at a nearby college, the University of Montevallo. A school bus provided transportation to and from the program. I remember being so excited for the first day of the program. Just that I was actually going to be on a college campus was huge for me. It was my first experience in a college environment. As I rode the bus to our first session,

I thought, "Okay, Liz. You are going to find out if you can hang with the big boys. Are you really cut out for this?" I was so nervous.

When we arrived on campus, I had butterflies. We began the session by taking a series of personality and interest profile tests so that we could learn what college majors fit us. I was pleased to learn that my test results were consistent with my goals of doing something in the legal field.

The program introduced us to the rigors of college-level courses. Through the program, I gained confidence in my potential to be successful in college. More importantly, the experience helped me overcome my insecurities about being a poor country girl from Clanton, Alabama. I found that I quickly made friends and that I had leadership skills.

When I returned to high school, I decided I would look into other summer college preparatory programs for the next summer. Of course, I didn't have the resources to pay for a program, so I needed something that targeted low-income or at-risk youth. I went to Mr. Steele, my Alabama history teacher, and he told me about the Minority Introduction to Engineering Program (MITE) at Auburn University.

The thought of a larger university like Auburn terrified me, but I mustered the courage to apply for the program. To my surprise, I was accepted. I would live on campus for a week in the residential dorms and attend courses in engineering.

My grandma gave me permission to go. So, I worked extra hours to save up money to purchase things that I would need for my weeklong stay. Auburn provided a list. As usual, I needed a ride. Auburn was more than 80 miles from Clanton. I was discussing my dilemma with my neighbor and friend, Lanette. Her older sister, Gwen, overheard me talking about it and offered to take me if I would cover her gas money. I was so thankful. I accepted her offer and made sure that I put some money aside for fuel.

I will never forget how I felt when I was dropped off for the MITE program. It reminded me so much of my first day of first grade. Although I was thankful to Gwen for driving, she just made sure that I got to the building that I needed to go to and dropped me off. The other students came with their parents who made sure that they were settled in. Like my first day of first grade, I had to read signs and navigate my way around to figure out where I needed to go. Like first grade, one of the program professors, Dr. Rod Jenkins, noticed my resourcefulness. He asked me how I got there, and I explained how I paid my neighbor gas money to bring me.

He said, "Well, Elizabeth Humphrey, you are certainly going to be a success. I hope Auburn gets you as a student."

Living up to Dr. Jenkins' prediction, I did well in the program and won awards at our closing ceremony. I left Auburn that summer confident that I could handle college.

Through my experiences at Upward Bound and Auburn, I learned that it was going to take more than making strainght "A"s to get me a college scholarship. I needed to make a good score on the college entrance exam. When school started back, I went to my guidance counselor and signed up to take the college entrance test. My test results were good, but they were not good enough for me to get the full scholarship that I would need.

I asked my computer teacher, Mrs. Huff, if she knew of any way that I could improve my scores.

She told me, "Sure, we have got some computer disks with programs on them to help you prepare for the test. Most students that use them improve their scores."

I replied, "Thank you so much, Mrs. Huff, but I can't take them because I don't have a computer at home."

She paused for a moment and said, "Let me see what I can do."

Later that same day, Mrs. Huff came to me and said, "I have arranged for you to be able to come into the computer lab and practice in the mornings before homeroom. I know you ride an early bus. So, if you use your time wisely, you should be able to get at least thirty minutes of practice in every morning."

I lit up and thought about how my prayers were answered once again. I hugged Mrs. Huff and thanked her for making the arrangements.

For six weeks, I went to the computer lab to practice each morning. It was hard because I enjoyed the school morning visits with my peers. I had to sacrifice that time for something more important. The sacrifice paid off, and I greatly improved my score on the test.

– 16 –

My senior year finally arrived and things could not be better. I was on track to be eligible for some great college scholarships and to be named one of the valedictorians of my senior class. All of the hard work had paid off. My happiness did not last long.

I came home from school one day and found my grandma sitting very still in the living room with a sad look on her face. Aunt Liz was there. I knew that my grandma had a doctor's appointment earlier that day. I asked, "Grandma, how did your doctor's appointment go?"

Aunt Liz started to cry and said, "She's got lung cancer."

I stood there frozen. After what seemed like several minutes, I asked, "Can't they do something for it? Can't they do chemo or something and fix it?"

Aunt Liz responded, "It's too far gone. There's nothing they can do."

My grandma did not say a word. It was as if she was not even in the room while we were having the conversation. I went on to ask the dreaded question, "How long are they giving her?"

Aunt Liz replied, "Months."

All I wanted to do at that moment was grab my grandma and hug her. I wanted to kiss her on the cheek and tell her I loved her. Knowing that my grandma was not an affectionate person, I refrained from reaching out to her. I regret that moment to this day.

Instead, I ran back to my room and sobbed in my pillow. I went through a series of emotions. First, I hurt for my grandma and wondered how long she knew she was sick. Then, I became angry that my grandma smoked cigarettes. And, finally, I became scared for my sister, her daughter Meghann, and myself. I got up out of the bed and went back to the front room and asked Aunt Liz, "What's going to happen to us?"

She replied, "I don't know. We are going to just have to take it one day at a time."

– 17 –

With the news of my grandma's illness, the excitement for my senior year was gone. I watched my grandma get worse each day. I really just went through the motions and was counting down the days to graduation.

One day I received an exciting package. I was invited to participate in the National Young Leaders Conference (NYLC). The conference would be held at Georgetown University in Washington, D.C. As excited as I was to have the opportunity, I knew that I could not go for two reasons. First, I did not want to leave my grandma for any extended period of time. And, second, there was no way that I could afford the more than three thousand dollar tuition to attend the program.

Although I had no intention of going, I was excited about the offer and shared my news with Annette Latham, a volunteer and board member at the local

YMCA. She was so proud of me and asked, "So when will you be going?"

I responded, "Mrs. Annette, you know I can't go with my grandma in her condition. And you know I don't have that kind of money."

She paused and said, "I'll bet if you reached out to the community, you could get the money for the tuition."

I responded, "Maybe so, Mrs. Annette, but I can't leave my—"

She interrupted me, "You need to go home and tell your grandma about this and see what she says. Don't tell her about the money part. I'll bet she would want you to go."

I replied, "But I feel guilty asking about something like this when she is in her condition."

Mrs. Annette continued, "Just tell her, Liz, and let me know what she says."

I went home after work that night and told Grandma about the NYLC opportunity.

She smiled and said, "Liz in Washington. Who would have thought?"

I responded, "I know it sounds good, Grandma, but I don't want to leave you."

She snapped back, "Don't you worry about me. You go ahead and go to Washington and make me proud."

I knew then that I needed to go.

I went to Mrs. Annette the next day and told her about my conversation with my grandma. She smiled and said, "That's what I thought would happen. Now, we need to raise that money."

I asked, "How am I going to raise that kind of money?"

She said, "I am going to help you write a letter to be put in the local newspaper asking for help to cover the tuition cost. You will be surprised."

We drafted the letter and placed it in the local paper. Mrs. Annette was right. I was pleasantly surprised. I raised all of the money that I needed to attend the conference. I was so excited. Everything fell in place for me to get to go. I even came home one day to find a very pleasant unexpected surprise. My paternal uncle Bradford came to visit my grandma and brought me a set of luggage. He told me that he knew I was going to need it for more than just the NYLC trip because he knew I was going places. I not only treasured the gift, more importantly I treasured the encouragement.

I remember sharing the news with Mrs. Annette. "We did it! We did it!" I ran in to tell her when I arrived to work at the YMCA after school.

She replied with her arms spread for a big hug, "I told you we would."

Suddenly, I stopped and pulled back from her and said, "I don't have any clothes and everything is going to be so fancy. There is even going to be a fancy dinner with evening gowns and everything!" I thought about the amount of money that I would need to purchase the type of clothes that would be appropriate to wear for this type of conference. I wondered if I could fit in with the kids that would attend since they were likely to come from wealthy families. I did not even know how to properly eat at a formal dinner.

Mrs. Annette put her hand on my shoulder and said, "Don't worry about it, we will get you ready."

A few weeks before the conference, Mrs. Annette told me that she needed me to come to her house one day after work. When we arrived at her beautiful home, she had a big surprise for me. We walked into her dining room, and she had the table set for a formal dinner. She sat me down and went through the different types of forks, spoons and knives and their uses. She explained why I had multiple beverage glasses and plates. It was all so confusing, and I was overwhelmed.

She gave me a book called *Miss Manners* and told me to study it carefully. She gave me some elegant wool dress suits to borrow because the weather in Washington would be cold. To wrap things up, she gave me some of the best advice that I have ever received. She said, "Liz, I know that you may be nervous and overwhelmed. I am confident that you are going to represent your city, county, and state well. Just always remember that, no matter where life takes you, there will always be someone in the room that knows what they are doing. Just relax and watch for that person. You will know them when you see them. Then, follow their lead." She gave me a hug and said, "You are going to do great."

Mrs. Annette was right. When I attended the conference, I followed her advice and watched the people in the room. There was always someone around who clearly knew what they were doing. And, as advised, I followed their lead.

The conference was a wonderful experience for me. It made me realize what had been said to me numerous times by my pastor. He constantly told me, "Elizabeth, you can be anything that you want to be and you can go anywhere you want to go. With God, all things are possible." And God used Mrs. Annette to get me ready.

– 18 –

Grandma's condition got so bad that the social workers discussed the possibility of putting Grandma in a nursing home for her care. My aunts and uncles were not going to allow my grandma to go to a nursing home. So, one of my aunts (Grandma's older daughter) moved from Detroit to live with us and take care of Grandma.

My aunt was a very attractive woman and maintained a glamorous appearance. She was very firm and very particular about how she wanted things done around the house. She liked for things to be exceptionally clean. She insisted that Grandma be handled a particular way.

My sister and I did not mind our aunt's pickiness at all because we were just thankful that we were able to stay together in our home with our grandma. We knew that it was just a matter of time for our grandma because her condition worsened daily. She lost a lot of weight and looked so fragile. She did not move around much, and she struggled to breathe. It was so painful to watch.

As the days passed, my relationship with my aunt became very strained. I was working two jobs and babysitting when needed. I was trying to save money for college and to pay for my "senior year" expenses. My aunt told me that I was not pulling my load and doing my share around the house. Although she was right to accuse me of rarely being home, I got angry at her because I did not understand why she was mad at me for working and doing extracurricular activities that would help me get to college. In hindsight, my actions probably did appear selfish to her. I wish that I could rewind the clock and explain to her what I was trying to accomplish and why it required so much of my time away from home. Maybe she would have understood.

One day, we bumped heads so bad that my aunt put me out of the house. She gave me an ultimatum, "Stay home today and help me take care of Mama or you need to get out!"

I had to go to school and work, so I left. When I returned from work, the argument that day was very loud and everyone in the neighborhood watched the spectacle. When she kicked me out, I ran up to Mildred's house. I explained to her what had happened, and she picked up the phone and said, "We are gonna call Daddy."

When my pastor got on the phone, I explained what had happened. I said, "I am so close to graduation and now because of this, my social workers will probably move me and I don't have any relatives to stay with in the county!" I sobbed and said, "I don't want to leave my home or my grandma!" As I cried out to him, it dawned on me that, at least at that moment, I was homeless and helpless.

My pastor listened and then said without hesitation, "You can come and live out here." He went on to say, "Tell Mildred to take you to get your stuff and bring you out here. We can deal with the authorities tomorrow."

At that moment, I was not sure how long he meant that I could stay. I just felt relieved that I had a place to go that did not require leaving my hometown. I wanted to stay near my grandma and finish high school in Clanton.

I handed Mildred the phone. She received her instructions and put her arm around me and said, "Let's go." She borrowed her brother Eli's truck and took me to the house to get my things. When we arrived, people in the neighborhood were standing outside watching. We put my stuff in plastic garbage bags and threw them into the back of the truck. My grandma was so sick that she was not even aware of what was going on.

When I arrived at my pastor's house, he and his wife were waiting for me at the door. They let me know that I could stay there as long as I needed to. His wife showed me to my room and let me know where I could find things that I would need. We did not say much to each other that night. There was no need. Their kindness said it all.

~ 19 ~

Although things were awkward with my biological family, I continued to live with my pastor and his wife. I made peace with my aunt, and she would let me go by the house and visit my grandma whenever I wanted. I missed my little Meghann so much. It was hard to live across town from them, but it was for the best.

Living with my pastor and his wife gave me much-needed stability. For the first time in my life, I lived in a home with a happily married couple. It was beautiful to watch how they worked together and gave so much of their time to help people. His wife was a great example to me of how a woman should carry herself. In the short time that I lived with them, I learned so many things.

The only downside to living with them was that they lived almost a fifteen- minute drive from town, and I did not have a car. My pastor and his wife only had one car that they shared. I had to rely on my boyfriend or friends to get around. My boyfriend, Keith Zeigler, was usually the only one that would drive that far out to get me. He even tried to coordinate his work schedule at Wal-Mart with mine so that he could give me a ride. My lack of transportation almost made me miss a great opportunity in school. But, as always, God provided.

When I attended the college summer programs, I learned that high school Advanced Placement (AP) courses were very helpful for college preparation. My high school did not offer any AP courses until my calculus teacher, Miss Linda Ellison, convinced my principal to let her teach a "crash course" for AP calculus. When she made the announcement about the AP class offering, I was so excited. Then, she explained that the principal said that she could offer the course only during the early morning hours before homeroom. There was no way for me to get to school on time for the class because the bus from my pastor's house got to school late and my pastor's wife would have their only car at work. "What a bummer!" I thought.

The next week, the AP class started and my peers that attended went on and on about how much they were learning. Within a few days after the AP class started, Miss Ellison called me to her desk during the regular school hours. She asked me why I was not taking the AP class. I explained my transportation problem to her. She said that she understood. The next day, she called me to her desk again and said, "I really think you can benefit from the AP course. So, I will pick you up from now on so that you can attend." I could not believe her act of kindness. Nor did I appreciate at the time what a sacrifice she made to help me.

I later learned that Miss Ellison drove almost 30 minutes to get to school every day, and she added an additional 25 minutes to her commute to pick me up for the early morning AP course. When I learned about her sacrifice, I broke down and cried. It meant so much to me that someone would do that for me. That is how God always took care of me. He touched the hearts of people like Miss Ellison to provide what was needed.

Once the course ended, we had to take a test. If we scored a certain score on the test, we could receive college credit. The sacrifice that Miss Ellison made to get me to the course made me want to let her know that her efforts were not in vain. I put in many long hours studying for the test. The hard work paid off and I, along with a few others, scored high enough to earn college credit. The look on her face when she gave us our scores was priceless. She wanted us to know that, although we were from a small rural school, we could handle college work. She accomplished her mission.

– 20 –

It was decision time. All of the years of sticking with school in spite of what was going on around me had paid off. I was named one of the valedictorians for my class, and I had scholarship offers from several schools. I felt like a highly sought-after athlete. I was so thankful.

Choosing a college was such a big decision for me. I needed to go to a college where I would feel comfortable. I had visited several schools and everyone had been so nice to me. As a first-generation college student, I had no clue what to look for in a college.

One day, I spread all of my scholarship letters across my bed. I just stood there staring at them trying to make a decision. Then, my pastor walked into my room. He asked, "What are you doing, Elizabeth?"

I said, “Pop, I don’t know what to do! There are so many to choose from. I don’t know which one is right for me.”

My pastor picked up one of the brochures and read aloud, “I believe in my country, because it is a land of freedom and because it is my own home and that I can best serve that country by ‘doing justly, loving mercy, and walking humbly with my God.’”

The passage caught my attention. I asked, “What are you reading?”

He replied, “Part of this school’s creed. It’s rare to find a school that stands for something like this.” I agreed, and he placed the brochure back on the bed. It was a brochure for Auburn University, and the passage he read came from their creed.

My pastor did not say another word and walked out the door. I sat down on my bed and read the entire Auburn Creed. My decision was made. I was going to accept the scholarship to Auburn. When I read the creed, I thought about how happy I was when I spent a week at the summer MITE program. It all made sense for me. I knew the campus. It was less than ninety miles from Clanton. One of my good friends, Randy Watts, was going to Auburn, so I would have a friend there and a way to get home if needed. A young lady from our sister church went there, and she had already let me know that she would love for me to come to Auburn.

I was so excited that I had finally made my decision. The next day, I went to one of my school guidance counselors to share my news. I thought that she was going to be so excited. I knew that she liked Auburn because both of her sons attended Auburn. I said to her, "Well, I finally made my decision. I am going to Auburn."

Her response shocked me. She said, "That's good, Elizabeth, but let's discuss that. I am concerned about someone like you attending such a big college right out of high school. It may be too overwhelming for you. Maybe you should consider asking Auburn to defer your scholarship for two years and stay here and get your college basics at the local community college and then go to Auburn. Because you don't have anybody to help you, I am scared for you to go down there right now."

Her words were crushing. For just a moment, her words actually made me pause and think about whether I could handle going to Auburn. Doubts began to flood my mind. Then, I looked at her and said, "No ma'am, I can't do that. It is now or never for me. I am getting out of here, and I will make it. God has got me this far, and I don't think that he's gonna leave me now."

She replied, "Well, you know that I wish nothing but the best for you." I walked out of her office and vowed that I would never step foot in there again.

I walked down the hall and back to my classroom. I kept saying over and over in my head, "God will take care of me."

Liz's senior portrait from school yearbook.

21

Graduation day finally arrived! I was so excited. Most of my peers were excited about their graduation trips to the beach. I was only excited about one thing—I made it. Although I had several scars from the hand that life had dealt me, I stood there in the doorway of my high school auditorium as one of the valedictorians of my class with a full scholarship to a great college. I looked down at the honor tassel and valedictorian medallion that hung from my neck, and tears filled my eyes.

My pastor and his wife arrived early so that they could sit on the front row. They were so proud of me. Several members of my biological family attended. But one thing made me sad; my grandma was not there. She was too weak to attend. We discussed putting her in a wheelchair to get her there, but we just were not able to make it work. As I sat on the stage and looked out at the audience, I imagined my grandma sitting there in one of her Sunday dresses with her purse clutched to her side and a smile on her face.

As soon as the ceremony was over and tons of pictures were taken, my friends jumped in their cars to head to the beach. I was only interested in going to one place. I went to see my grandma. When I walked into the house in my cap and gown, she smiled. I cried and bent down and hugged her. I pressed my face next to hers and said, "Grandma, I made it. Thank you for all that you did for me."

Although usually not affectionate, Grandma kissed me on my check and said, "Baby, I am so proud of you. Now, go out there and make something good of yourself." She went on to say, "Remember, people may have more stuff than you, but they are not smarter than you. I know you can do anything that you set your mind to do. You are smart, Elizabeth."

As I sat with her, I did not realize that I was having one of the last conversations with my grandma. She died at the end of my first semester at Auburn. Seeing her so fragile hurt me deeply. After all, this was the strong woman that had single-handedly raised eight children and two grandchildren. The tough skin on her hands revealed the years of manual labor that she did to provide for her family. She was a resourceful woman who did the best she could with what she had. She had given up her personal life and pleasures for her children. She had the strength to leave a marriage tainted by violence to protect them. I do not recall her doing anything special for herself. Occasionally, her sons, Bradford and Paul, would visit and insist on doing something nice for her.

She was so proud of the accomplishments of her children and grandchildren. It was as if their success gave her life meaning. And, unfortunately, for those of them that failed, their failures gave her great heartache. However, regardless of what her children did, she remained hopeful that they would take a turn for the best. Although she may have enabled some bad behaviors for her children because they knew that she would bail them out, she couldn't help herself. Her children, my sister, and I were her life. I loved her dearly.

– 22 –

I lay in my bed that night full of so many thoughts and emotions. A new and scary, but exciting chapter in life was about to begin for me. I would no longer have to "live with" and "bear through" the circumstances that I was born into. It was a new beginning.

I was nervous about leaving my hometown and church family because the people in my community knew me and they supported me. I will forever be grateful for the way God used my community and all the people around me to change the course of my life. Clanton was and is still today a predominantly white town. When I was growing up, less than ten percent of the community was black. Nevertheless, God showed me a loving humanity that transcended racial divides, that overcame the obstacles of a segregated community and the pitfalls of an integrated school.

I wondered, "Would people at Auburn respond to me the way that the people in my hometown had done all of my life?" Then I thought, "Of course they will." I realized that it was God that had loved me through all those people during my school years. And, I knew in my heart that He would continue to use people to guide and love me through this next chapter of life.

I got out of bed and began to make a list of the things I would need for school so that I could focus on purchasing a few items each time I got a paycheck that summer. I decided that I would plan to spend a night with my church sister, Vonnie McAfee, who attended Auburn. I would be living in the same on-campus apartments that she lived in and could learn more about what I needed with an overnight visit in the apartments. I also decided that I would move into my place as early as allowed before classes so that I could identify my class locations on campus and purchase my books before the campus was bustling with more than twenty thousand students. I had to take advantage of the resources in order to prepare myself.

Although striking out on my own was scary, I thought about the sermon that had given me the hope that God would always make a way for me. If God provided for the birds, then He would certainly provide for me because *I am more than a bird*.

Epilogue

After High School

I could write an entire new book about my college and law school experiences. Instead, I can just sum those years up with one statement: God continued to provide a way.

My pastor continued to provide me with emotional and spiritual support. If I did not catch a ride home for the weekend to attend church, my pastor and I would at least talk by phone. As for family, my paternal uncles Paul and Bradford were always available by phone with words of encouragement and would occassionally send me a nice letter with some money. My aunt Liz would make sure that I came to her house each year for Thanksgiving dinner.

At Auburn, as throughout my childhood years, the right people were put in my path. For example, my church sister, Vonnie, introduced me to the Tigerette program at Auburn. The Tigerettes were the official hostesses for Auburn football prospects. The director of the Tigerette program was Sue Locklar, who became a surrogate mother to me and was a huge support. I was also active in the Student Government Association (SGA). Thanks to the encouragement and mentoring from the then Vice President of Student Affairs, Grant Davis, and his wife, Nancy, I went as far as to run for SGA President.

Then, there was Auburn head football coach, Pat Dye. I got to know Coach Dye by serving as the Tigerette who worked directly with him on football Saturdays to meet and greet the top football recruits when they spent time with him in his office. While waiting on the recruits to show up, Coach Dye and I would talk about everything from football to life. We became so close that when I ran for SGA President, he actually introduced me for my speech in front of the student body.

God used my relationship with Coach Dye to help me at a critical turning point in my college experience. When I lost the SGA presidential election, I was uncertain about my future. I thought that I needed to win the election to put myself in a position to get into a good law school and get noticed by big law firms. I did not know what to do. Several days after the election, Coach Dye called me to his office to check on me. I told him about my concerns for my future.

He said, "Liz, how you deal with failure will define you. Anybody can do well when everything is going good. But it takes a person with strong character to pull themselves up when they fall down in life." He went on, "You just fell down, now you've got to pull yourself back up." He then asked, "What do you want to do with your life after college?"

I replied, "I want to go to law school and become a successful lawyer."

He asked, "How do you know you want to be a lawyer? Do you know any lawyers? Law school takes a lot of time and money for you to just do it and not be sure."

I replied, "I only know a few lawyers from my small town, and I know Nancy Davis. I have never spent any time in a law firm environment."

He ended the conversation with, "Well, you need to think about that."

A few days later, I was working in the Tigerette office, and Coach Dye's secretary called me and told me that she had something for me. I went to her office and she handed me a torn-off piece of paper with a man's name and phone number on it. She said, "Coach Dye told me to give you this and said for you to call this person. He said that you will know what it's about."

Although I replied, "Yes, ma'am," I really did not know what it was about. I immediately went to give the man named Sam Franklin a call. Sam was a founding partner in a well-respected law firm in Birmingham, Alabama called Lightfoot, Franklin & White.

When Sam answered the phone, I said, "Hello, Mr. Franklin, my name is Liz Humphrey, and Coach Pat Dye told me to call you."

He replied with the nicest southern gentleman accent that I had ever heard, "Well, hello, Liz. Coach Dye has told me all about you. I understand you want to be a lawyer."

"Yes, sir," I replied.

He went on, "Well, if you would like, we have arranged for you to come and spend the summer with our law firm so that you can find out if you really like the practice of law. We have arranged for you to stay with a Cumberland law student. It's all taken care of if you would like to come."

Tears began to roll down my face. I could not believe that I was being given this opportunity. I swallowed hard so that he would not hear me crying and said, "Yes, sir. I would love to." The summer experience at Lightfoot certainly confirmed for me that I wanted to practice law. And, it's amazing how things come full circle; I am now an attorney at Lightfoot.

Once I was certain about going to law school, I began to focus on studying for the law school entrance exam called the LSAT. I discussed studying for the exam with my peers that were also preparing for the exam and learned that they were taking an LSAT prep course. I wanted to take the prep course because I knew how much it would help me, but I just could not afford the $800 fee. As I was studying one day, Randy, my friend from Clanton, asked me how things were going. I told him that I was working as hard as I could, but really wished that I could afford to take that prep course. Later that night, Randy came to my apartment and said, "I talked to my parents today, and my dad wants you to call him."

Randy's dad, Randol Watts, was and still is a dear person with a kind heart. I called him and he said, "Now listen here, youngun'. You need to take that course and Joann and I want to help. Randy has my credit card, and I want you to use it to pay for the course."

I replied, "Thank you so much, Mr. Watts, but I can't repay that type of money."

He said, "This is not a loan. This is an investment. Now I am telling you to register for the course."

I knew that he was not going to take no for an answer, so I said, "Yes, sir." Once again, God used someone to be a game-changer for me.

While in college, I did not just grow into a woman. I earned the distinction of becoming an Auburn woman. I also gained something else from Auburn—an Auburn man. I met my dear husband, Tony Huntley, at Auburn after I had graduated. Our relationship blossomed instantly, and we are now happily married with three beautiful children. It is such a blessing to watch my children grow up in a stable home.

After college, I had the privilege to work as an intern for a non-profit education reform organization called A+, The Coalition for Better Education. I learned so much during the year of my internship. I got to travel the state and work with so many outstanding leaders. Two of those leaders were Bobby Segall and Alyce Spruell. They were both attorneys, and I spoke with them at length about law school. Alyce was the Associate Dean at the University of Alabama School of Law. She invited me to visit the law school and observe classes. While there, I saw several of my college peers. After interacting with several of the faculty members, I knew that it was the perfect fit for me. And, to top it off, I received a partial scholarship. So, once again, God had provided a way, and I received an outstanding law school education.

Through my life experiences, I have learned that God can bless anyone with a life as a contributing member of society. Even if a person is born into terrible circumstances like I was, God can provide the resources needed for success. If He provides for the birds, He will certainly provide for us. But like the birds, we have to do our part to get what we need. Birds do not sit in one place and wait for someone to come along and feed them. They take action and go where they need to go to be fed knowing that something will be provided. People put out bird baths and feeders because they know that birds will use them. Likewise, people are willing to help those who will help themselves. I hope that this book will inspire you to take those steps to take advantage of the opportunities that God presents us with each day to have a good quality of life.

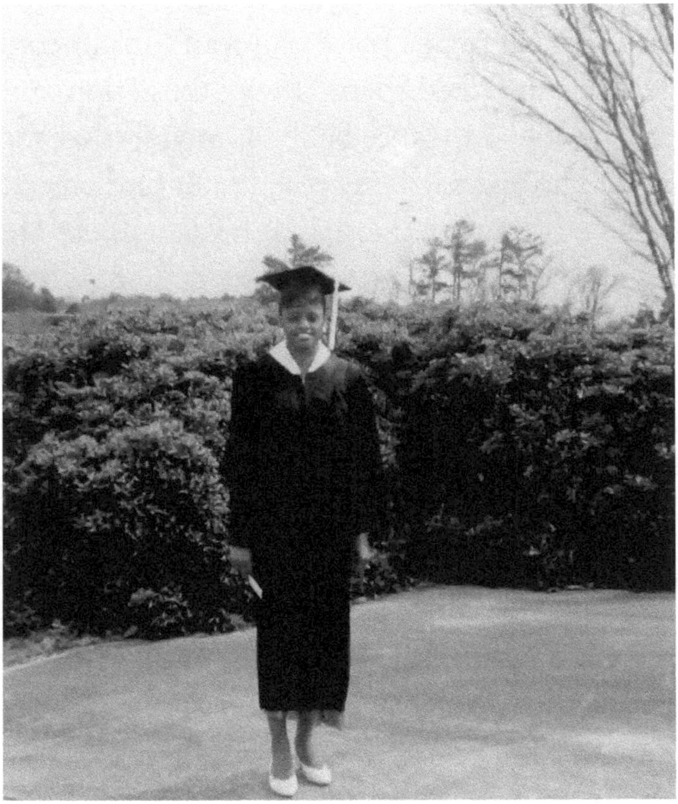

Liz on college graduation day.

CPSIA information can be obtained
at www.ICGtesting.com
Printed in the USA
LVHW02s1600220818
587764LV00022B/874/P

9 780692 492031